How to Draw SUPERHEROES and SUPER VILLAINS

WRITTEN AND ILLUSTRATED BY SCOTT BOOTH

DESIGNED BY BILL HENDERSON

PUBLISHED BY TANGERINE PRESS, AN IMPRINT OF SCHOLASTIC INC, 557 BROADWAY, NEW YORK, NY 10012

10 9 8 7 6 5 4 3 2 1

ISBN 0-439-55133-1

PRINTED AND BOUND IN CHINA

How to Draw
SUPERHEROES
and SUPER VILLAINS

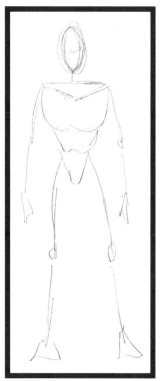
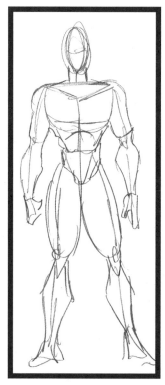
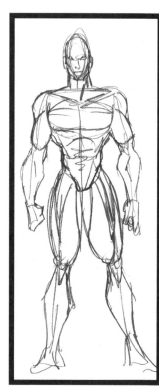

WELCOME TO HOW TO DRAW SUPERHEROES AND SUPER VILLAINS. HERE'S WHERE YOU'LL LEARN TO DRAW YOUR OWN CHARACTERS. ALL YOU NEED IS A PENCIL AND PLAIN WHITE PAPER TO GET STARTED.

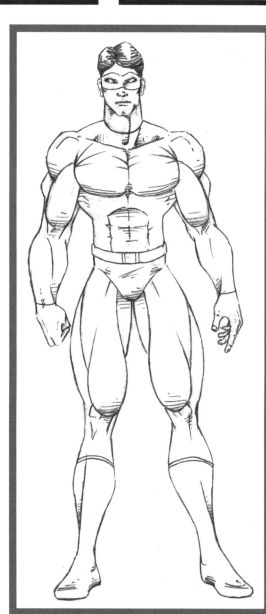

START BY LIGHTLY SKETCHING A BASIC HUMAN SKELETON. USE AN OVAL FOR THE HEAD AND STRAIGHT LINES FOR THE BONES. NEXT, LIGHTLY SKETCH THE FORM OF THE ARMS, BODY, AND LEGS.

THEN, DEFINE THE MUSCLES. IN THE NEXT FEW PAGES, YOU'LL SEE HOW THE MUSCULAR SYSTEM IS PUT TOGETHER.

NOW, REFINE THE MUSCLE DETAILS. LIGHTLY ERASE SKETCH LINES. YOU WILL STILL BE ABLE TO SEE THE FORM OF YOUR CHARACTER. FINALLY, GO OVER THE ERASED IMAGE WITH A DARK, CRISP, CLEAN LINE.

TO COMPLETE YOUR CHARACTER AND MAKE IT LOOK 3D, YOU'LL NEED TO ADD SHADING. DECIDE WHERE THE LIGHT IS COMING FROM AND SHADE ON THE OPPOSITE SIDE. ALSO, SHADE WHERE THE MUSCLES ROLL UNDER OR AROUND THE BODY.

FINALLY, ADD COSTUME DETAILS LIKE A MASK, CAPE, OR SYMBOLS, AND JUST LIKE THAT YOU'VE CREATED A CHARACTER! IF YOU GET STUCK, LOOK AT OTHER SUPERHERO COMICS TO SEE HOW THE PROS DO IT.

BODY OPTIONS

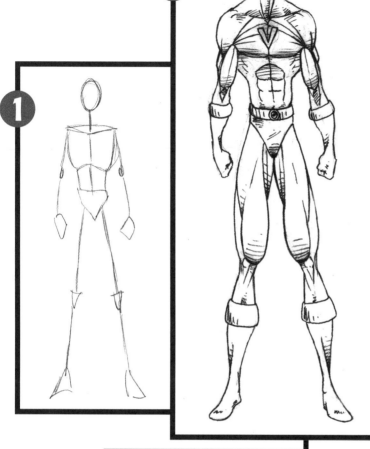

Bodies come in all shapes and sizes, and so to super-heroes. First, start with the same basic skeleton. Define the muscles of the body, arms, and legs. Keep this character thin. Erase the sketch lines, leaving the guidelines. Define the character's shape with a dark line. Finally, add a costume and some shading to create this lean, mean superhero.

Now try drawing a muscular character. These heroes are usually the biggest and the strongest. Begin by drawing the same basic skeleton. Next, add the basic muscle outline of the arms, legs, and body. This time make the muscles huge. Now, add definition to the muscles and erase the guidelines. Go over the lines with a dark, crisp line. Add some shading and a costume.

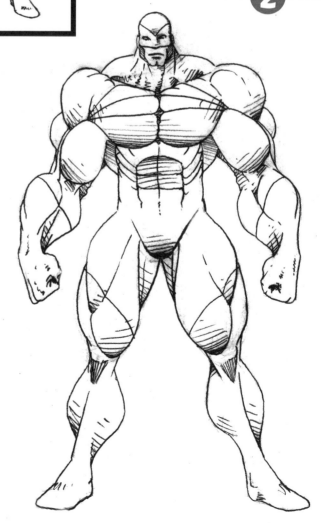

TORSO MUSCLES

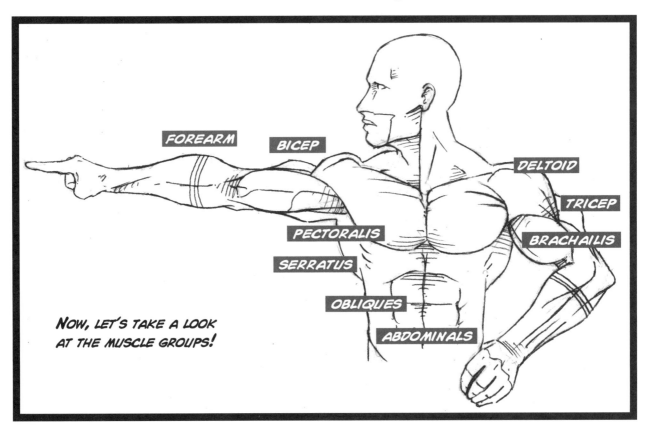

FOREARM

BICEP

DELTOID

TRICEP

PECTORALIS

BRACHAILIS

SERRATUS

OBLIQUES

ABDOMINALS

NOW, LET'S TAKE A LOOK AT THE MUSCLE GROUPS!

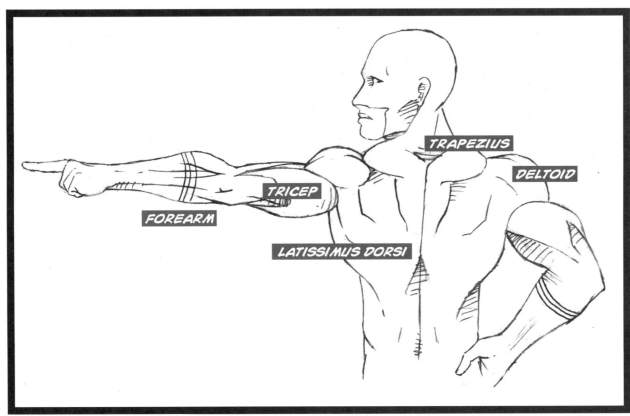

TRAPEZIUS

DELTOID

TRICEP

FOREARM

LATISSIMUS DORSI

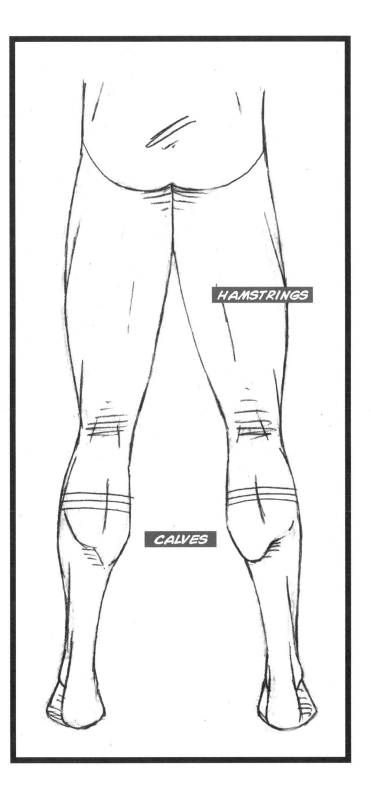

HAMSTRINGS

CALVES

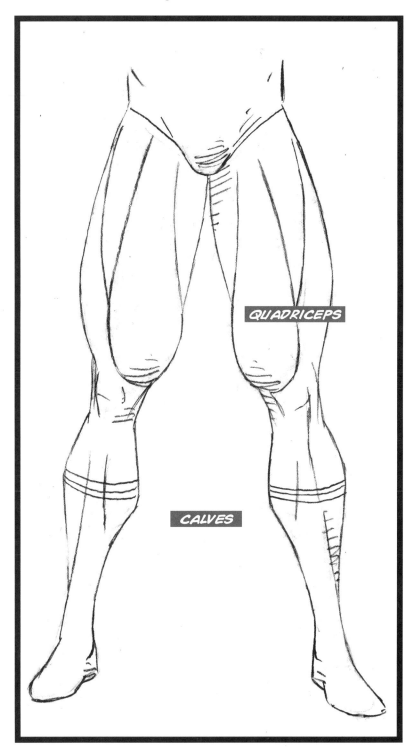

QUADRICEPS

CALVES

THE FACE

Now that you know the steps for creating a basic super hero, add a little more detail to the face. Start by drawing an oval shape for the head. Then, lightly draw a line horizontally and vertically, through the middle of the oval. These are the guidelines for the facial features.

Next, draw bean-shaped ovals for the eyes. Make sure they are equal distance from the vertical line. Place a triangle for the nose on the horizontal line, taking up almost half the bottom part of the vertical line. Sketch a line to indicate the mouth and the chin crossing the vertical line. (See figure 2.)

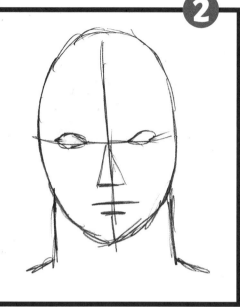

1

2

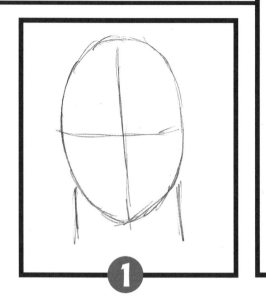

3

4

Next, refine the facial features by adding a curved line at the bottom of the nose triangle. Add the ears, starting at the eye line and ending about where the nose ends. Add the cheek bones with an outward curving line that starts on the outline of the head and cuts in toward the mouth. Sketch the chin at the bottom of the oval. Indicate the forehead with a small line. Now, lightly erase the guidelines. Draw over the guidelines with a dark line, and add some shading and costume details. Now, check out your cool character!

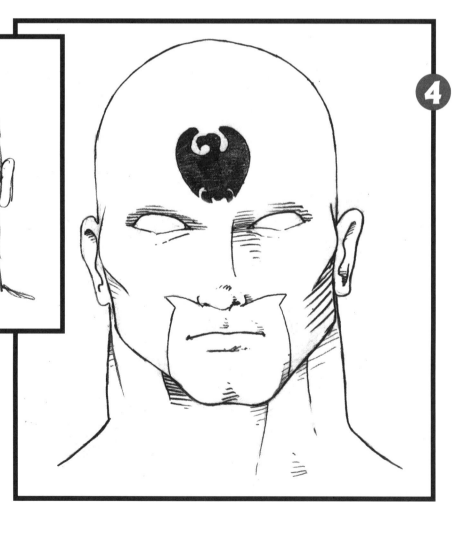

FACE OPTIONS

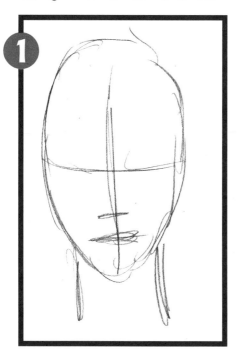

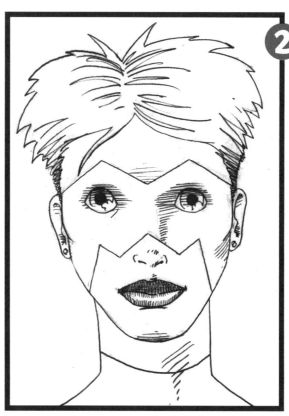

2 FACES COME WITH DIFFERENT SHAPES AND FACIAL FEATURES. START WITH THE OVAL HEAD AND LINES FOR THE EYES, NOSE, AND MOUTH. REFINE ALL OF THE FEATURES AS YOU DID ON PAGE 3. LIGHTLY ERASE THE GUIDELINES. GO OVER THE ERASED LINES WITH A DARK, CLEAN LINE. FINALIZE ALL OF THE FEATURES. ADD MORE SHADING AROUND THE CHIN, EYE SOCKETS, NOSE, AND WHERE THE FACE CURVES TO THE SIDES.

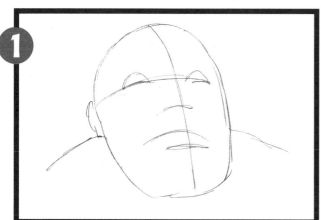

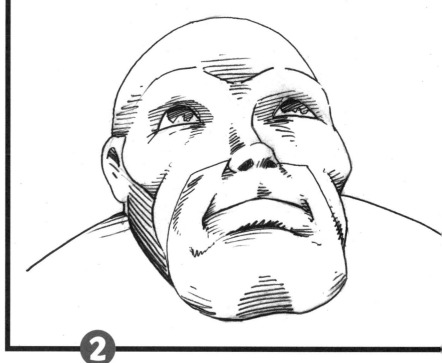

TRY WHAT YOU'VE LEARNED ABOUT DRAWING FACES WITH ONE THAT IS AT A DIFFERENT ANGLE. THIS SAMPLE FACE (FIGURE 2) ALSO HAS A LARGER JAW. START BY DRAWING A TILTED OVAL AND THE GUIDELINES FOR THE EYES, NOSE, AND MOUTH WITH A SLIGHT CURVE TO THEM. DEFINE THE CHARACTERISTICS OF THE FACE AND ERASE THE GUIDELINES. NOW, ADD THE DETAILS TO THE EYES, NOSE, MOUTH, CHIN, AND FOREHEAD. ADD THE COSTUME DETAILS AND SOME SHADING AS YOU DID BEFORE. YOU'VE CREATED ANOTHER SUPERHERO!

FEMALE STRUCTURE

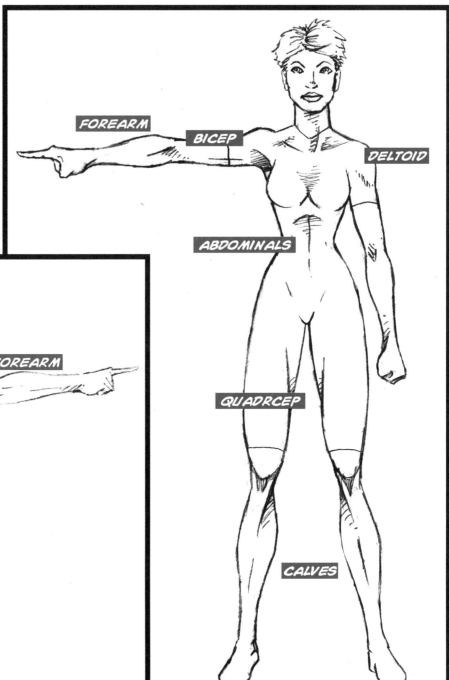

FOREARM

BICEP

DELTOID

ABDOMINALS

QUADRCEP

CALVES

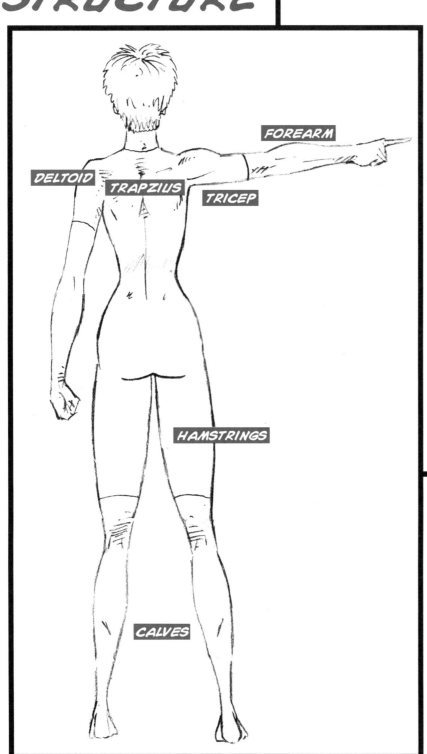

DELTOID

TRAPZIUS

FOREARM

TRICEP

HAMSTRINGS

CALVES

CAPTAIN ODO

As a small boy, Carlos was struck by a meteor fragment while he was fishing, but instead of harming him, it gave him the powers of the universe. Carlos gained the ability to fly at the speed of a comet, and has the strength of a thousand planets. Odo's mission is to always help the less fortunate, thwarting all evil-doer's plans.

Height: **6'2"**

Weight: **220 lbs.**

Press: **800 lbs.**

Birthplace: **Rio de Janeiro, Brazil**

Alignment: **Good**

Alias: **Carlos Araujo**

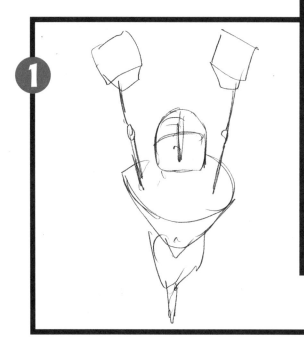

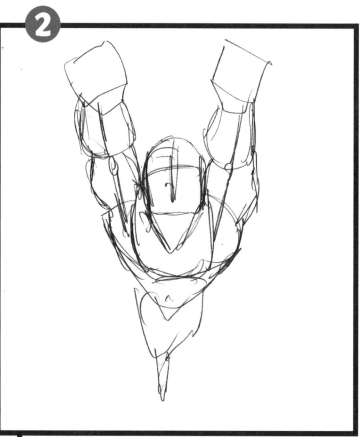

Draw the basic skeleton as if Captain Odo is flying at you. This is called foreshortening (to distort the lines to create an illusion of depth). Outline the muscles of the arms and upper body.

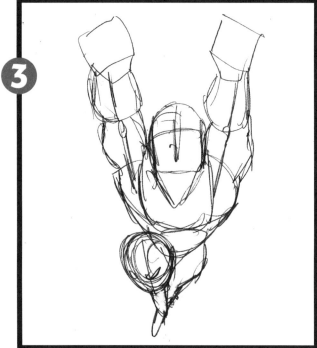

Outline the legs and thighs, and add a basic face guidelines. Define the fists, arms, and muscles of the body.

5

6

Now define the leg muscles and add the knee cap and feet. Next, erase the foundation of the fists and arms. Finalize these with dark, clean lines. Add some shading to give this area a 3D effect.

7

Refine the face and head with more detail. Once you feel comfortable with your drawing, erase the guidelines. Finalize the features with a dark line. Finally, erase the preliminary sketch of the legs and finalize them with clean lines. Remember, keep the drawing as neat as possible.

CAPTAIN ODO

1

NOW, PUT CAPTAIN ODO IN SOME DIFFERENT POSES. START BY DRAWING THE BASIC SKELETON WITH AN OVAL HEAD. DEFINE THE MUSCLES AND FACIAL FEATURES. ONCE YOU LIKE THE GUIDELINES, ERASE AND FINALIZE THE BODY. DON'T FORGET TO ADD THE COSTUME DETAILS AND THE SHADOWS.

2

1

FOR THIS POSE, START BY SKETCHING THE BASIC SKELETON AND ADD THE MUSCLES AS YOU DID BEFORE. DEFINE THE FACIAL FEATURES AND FISTS. ERASE THE GUIDELINES, AND CLEAN UP THE DRAWING WITH CRISP, DARK LINES. FINALIZE THE DRAWING WITH SOME SHADING AND THE COSTUME.

2

WARPATH

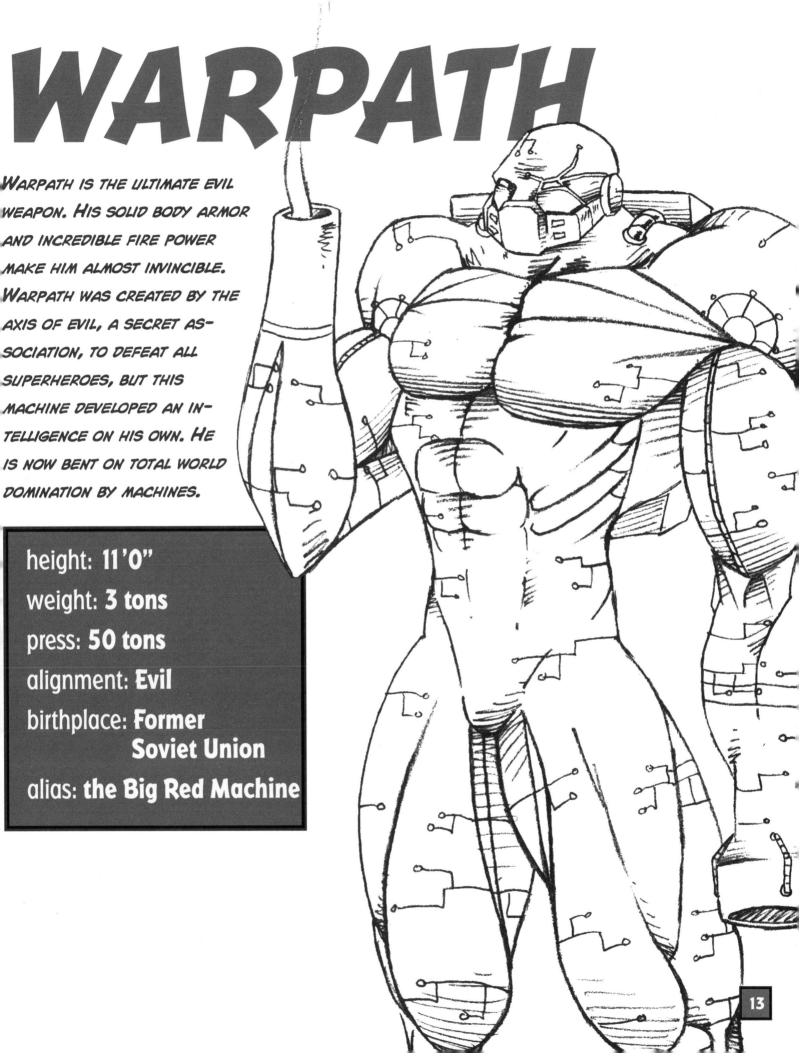

WARPATH IS THE ULTIMATE EVIL WEAPON. HIS SOLID BODY ARMOR AND INCREDIBLE FIRE POWER MAKE HIM ALMOST INVINCIBLE. WARPATH WAS CREATED BY THE AXIS OF EVIL, A SECRET AS-SOCIATION, TO DEFEAT ALL SUPERHEROES, BUT THIS MACHINE DEVELOPED AN IN-TELLIGENCE ON HIS OWN. HE IS NOW BENT ON TOTAL WORLD DOMINATION BY MACHINES.

height: **11'0"**
weight: **3 tons**
press: **50 tons**
alignment: **Evil**
birthplace: **Former Soviet Union**
alias: **the Big Red Machine**

TRY DRAWING WARPATH IN HIS MEN-
ACING POSE. BEGIN WITH THE BASIC
SKETCH. THEN DEFINE THE WEAPON
ON HIS FOREARM. NEXT, DEFINE
THE MUSCLES, MAKING THEM VERY
LARGE. (SEE PAGE 4)

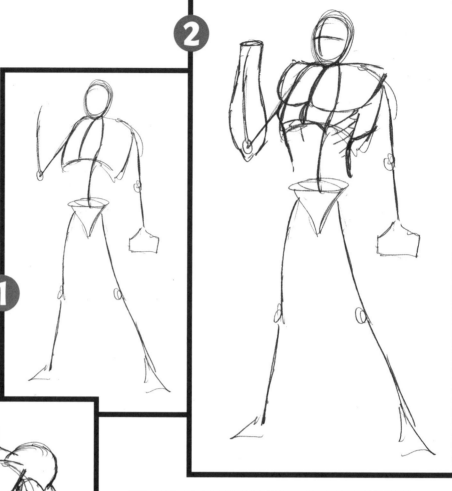

NOW, DEFINE THE MUSCLES IN THE ARMS AND
SHOULDERS, EXAGGERATING THE SIZE OF THE
MUSCLES. NEXT, DEFINE THE LEG MUSCLES, AGAIN
MAKING THEM LARGER THAN ON OTHER CHARAC-
TERS.

6

NOW, CLEAN UP THE IMAGE BY ERASING GUIDE-LINES AND DEFINING THE ABDOMINAL MUSCLES. ADD SOME LINES TO DEFINE THE PECTORALS (CHEST) AND DELTOIDS (SHOULDER). (SEE PAGE 6-8 FOR MUSCLE LOCATION)

5

THEN ERASE THE FOUNDATION LINES AND DEFINE THE IMAGE. KEEP THE LINES CLEAN AND DARK. ADD THE COSTUME ELEMENTS. THEN, ADD THE CIRCUITRY AND WIRING THAT KEEPS WARPATH OPERATING. ADD THE FINAL TOUCHES WITH SOME SHADING TO MAKE YOUR CHARACTER THREE-DIMENSIONAL.

7

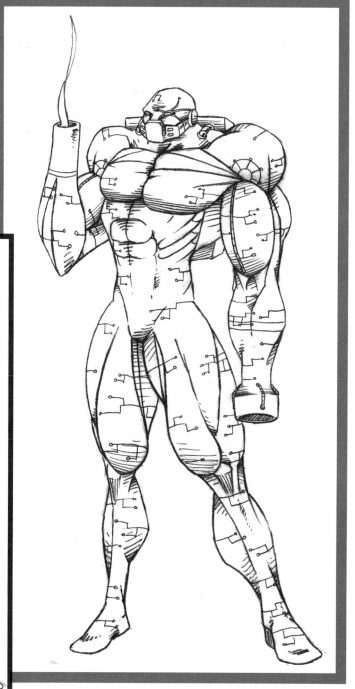

WARPATH

Try to draw Warpath in other poses. Here he is squatting, ready to leap. Follow the same steps as the preceding pages, starting with the basic skeleton.

1

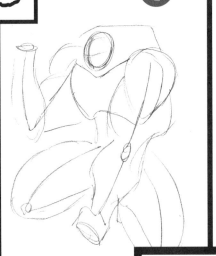

2

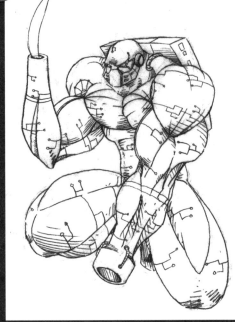

1

2

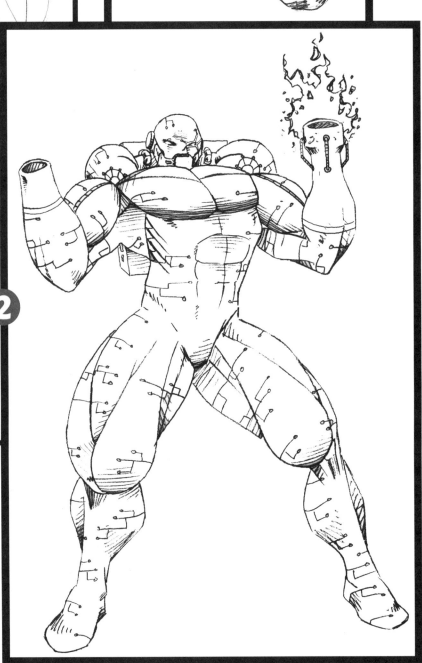

Now try Warpath in this position. Here he stands poised for attack.

HELIX

Helix was created when a genetic experiment with superhuman DNA went wrong. Kevin Wiegand, the world-renowned geneticist, was working on a way to help cure muscular diseases when his lab was struck by lightning, forever changing him into Helix. Helix has incredible strength, speed, and agility; combined with his martial arts skills, he's one tough hero.

height: **6'8"**

weight: **280 lbs.**

press: **1200 lbs.**

birthplace: **Florida, USA**

alignment: **Good**

alias: **Kevin Wiegand**

DRAW HELIX IN A MARTIAL ARTS POSE, STARTING WITH THE BASIC SKELETON, AS YOU DID WITH THE OTHER CHARACTERS. THEN, DEFINE THE MUSCLES OF THE ARMS AND BODY.

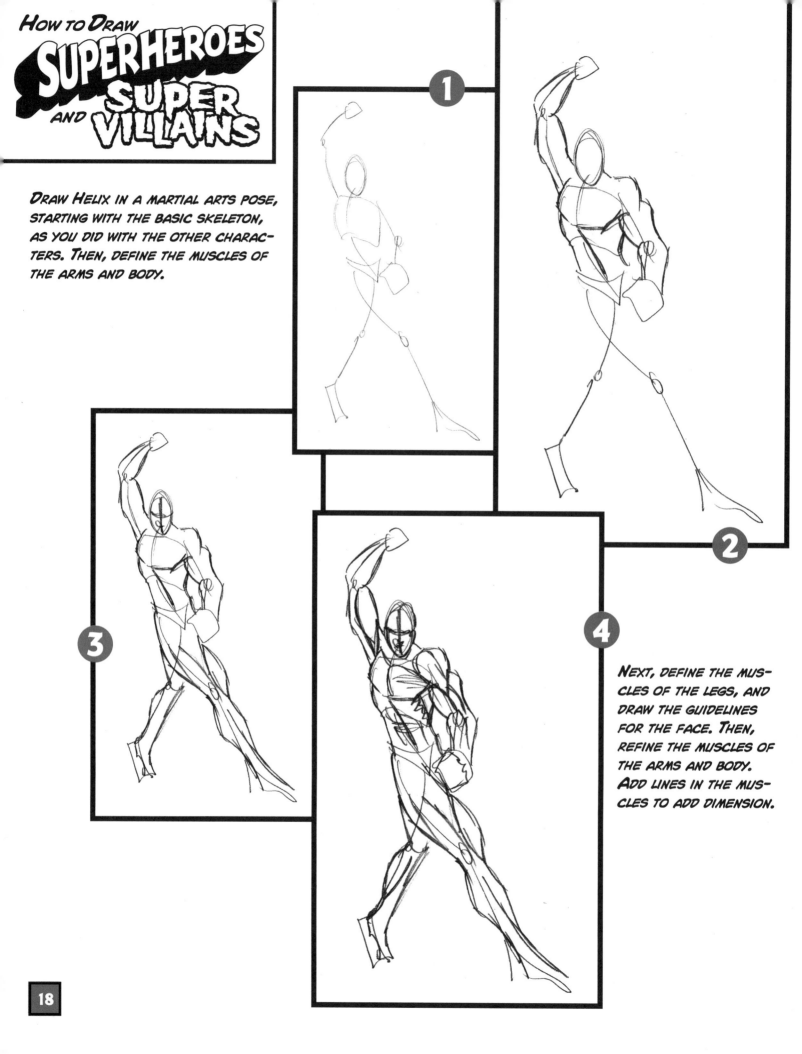

NEXT, DEFINE THE MUSCLES OF THE LEGS, AND DRAW THE GUIDELINES FOR THE FACE. THEN, REFINE THE MUSCLES OF THE ARMS AND BODY. ADD LINES IN THE MUSCLES TO ADD DIMENSION.

5

6

Now, refine the hands and fists, and add the facial features. Next, add some action lines to show movement on his right arm. Erase the guidelines on the right arm and face. Finalize these areas with dark, crisp lines.

7

Erase the foundation sketch on the left arm and torso. Define the abdominals and serratus muscles (see page 6-8). Add some lines for shading. Finally, erase the guidelines for the legs, and clean up the lower torso. Add some more shading, and finalize the drawing with a costume.

HELIX

Try drawing Helix in another martial arts pose. Pay special attention to the perspective for this pose. Follow the steps from previous pages, starting with basic skeleton.

1

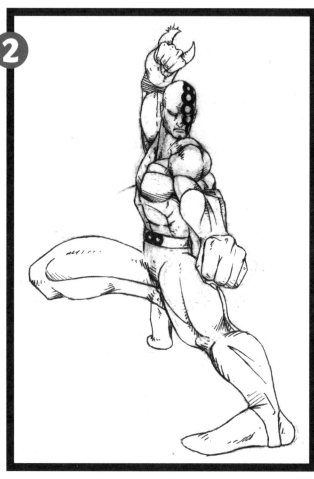

2

1

2

Now try a completely different pose with more angles. As always, start with the basic skeleton to show the position of the character's features. Next, use guidelines to define the face. Add muscles to the arms and body. Erase the foundation sketch, and finalize the drawing with dark, clean lines. Finally, add the costume and shading to finish your drawing.

CENTURIAN

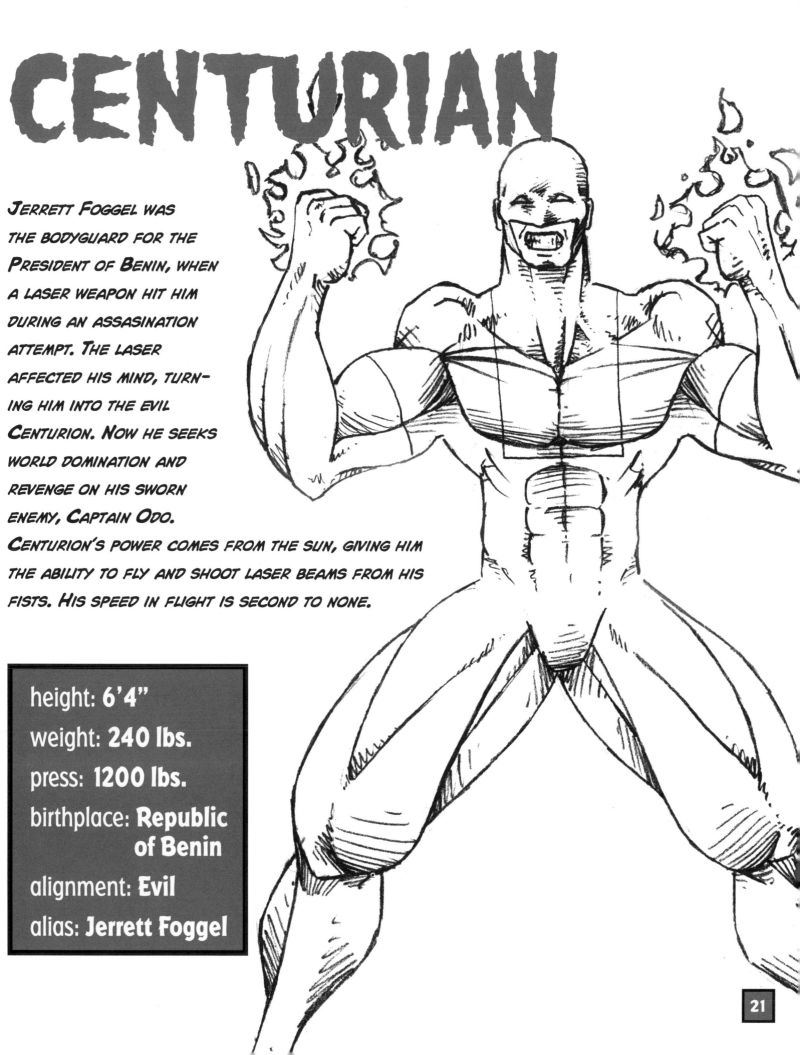

JERRETT FOGGEL WAS THE BODYGUARD FOR THE PRESIDENT OF BENIN, WHEN A LASER WEAPON HIT HIM DURING AN ASSASINATION ATTEMPT. THE LASER AFFECTED HIS MIND, TURNING HIM INTO THE EVIL CENTURION. NOW HE SEEKS WORLD DOMINATION AND REVENGE ON HIS SWORN ENEMY, CAPTAIN ODO.

CENTURION'S POWER COMES FROM THE SUN, GIVING HIM THE ABILITY TO FLY AND SHOOT LASER BEAMS FROM HIS FISTS. HIS SPEED IN FLIGHT IS SECOND TO NONE.

height: **6'4"**
weight: **240 lbs.**
press: **1200 lbs.**
birthplace: **Republic of Benin**
alignment: **Evil**
alias: **Jerrett Foggel**

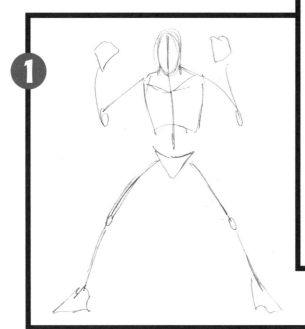

Draw Centurion as he gains energy from the sun. First, define the figure with the basic skeleton. Then, define the muscles of the body, arms, and shoulders.

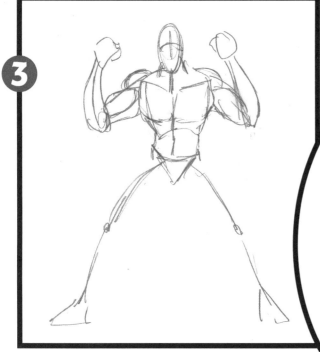

Now, refine the muscles of the arms and forearms. Finish defining the muscles of the legs and feet.

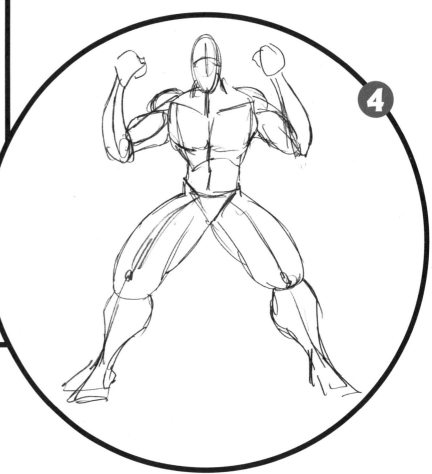

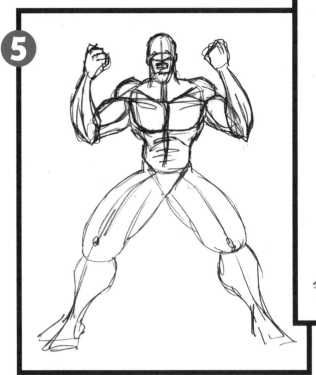

5

6

Draw the guidelines for the face, and sketch the basic facial features. Next, refine the muscles of the arms, legs, and body. Make sure you define the quadriceps.

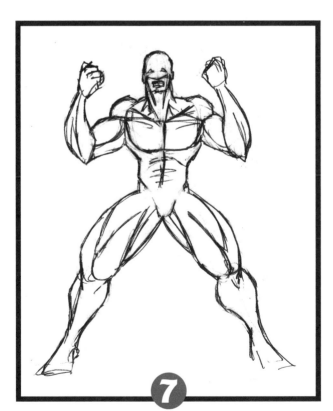

7

Now, clean up the image and make any final adjustments to the muscle structure. Erase the foundation sketch and finalize the image with clean lines. Add some shading, the costume, and the solar flares coming from his fists.

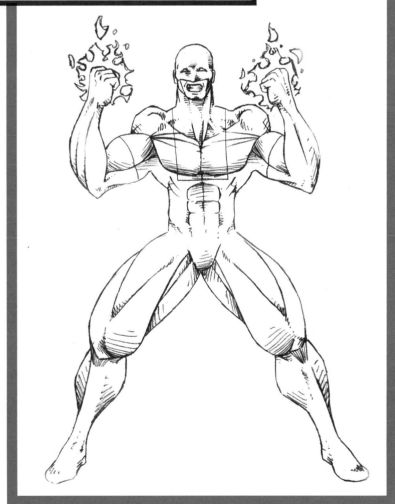

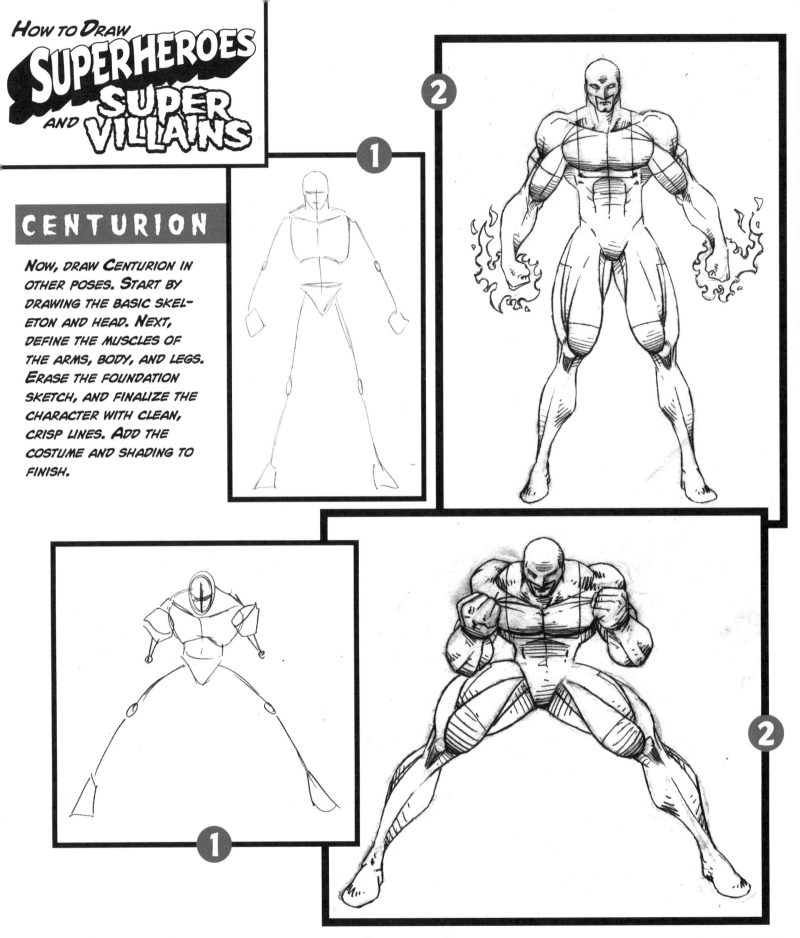

CENTURION

Now, draw Centurion in other poses. Start by drawing the basic skeleton and head. Next, define the muscles of the arms, body, and legs. Erase the foundation sketch, and finalize the character with clean, crisp lines. Add the costume and shading to finish.

Next, draw Centurion ready to attack. Begin by drawing the basic skeleton and guidelines of the face. Then, define the body, arm, and leg muscles. Erase the sketch, and finalize the drawing with clean, dark lines. Finally, add the costume and shading.

TITANIA

Titania was born on the Flusia Fjord over 1000 years ago. She is believed to be the daughter of the last great viking king. It is thought that she has survived by the use of magic and potions. An admitted alchemist, she uses her magic to perform all kinds of unbelievable feats. Titania has the ability to levitate, make herself invisible, and walk through walls. Her greatest ability is the power of telekinesis (the power to move things with her mind).

Height: **5'10"**
Weight: **135 lbs.**
Press: **100 lbs.**
Birthplace: **Norway**
Alignment: **Good**
Alias: **Titania Jorgensen**

HOW TO DRAW SUPERHEROES AND SUPER VILLAINS

START BY DRAWING TITANIA IN AN ACTION POSE. BEGIN BY DRAWING THE BASIC SKELETON IN THE POSITION YOU WISH. NEXT, DEFINE THE TORSO AND ARM MUSCLES. DRAW THE GUIDELINES FOR THE FACE.

THEN DRAW THE MUSCLES OF THE WAIST AND LEGS. NOW, SKETCH THE FACIAL FEATURES AND COSTUME. REFINE THE TORSO AND HAIR.

Now, erase the foundation sketching of the face and hair. Clean up these areas with crisp lines. Do the same thing for the shoulders and torso. Add some lines for shading.

Finish the arms and legs by erasing the the foundation lines. Clean up these areas by using dark, crisp lines. Finish any of the costume elements and shading. Now Titania is ready for battle.

T I T A N I A

Now, draw Titania in other poses. Try this pensive pose, starting with a basic skeleton.

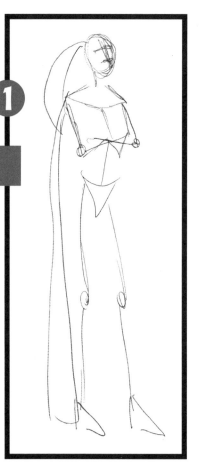

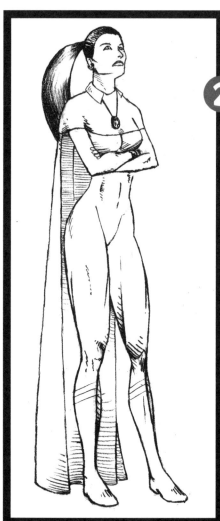

Now, draw Titania in an action pose. Begin with the basic human skeleton. Draw guidelines for the face, and add the muscle mass. Then erase and refine the form with clean lines. Add the final touches to the costume and shading. Now, Titania is ready for action.

APEX

Apex, the acrobat, was trained as a gymnast, trapeze artist, and a contortionist. His evil activities are fueled by his lust for money and power. His sworn enemy is the Changeling. They were both part of the same traveling circus. But now, they are bitter enemies.

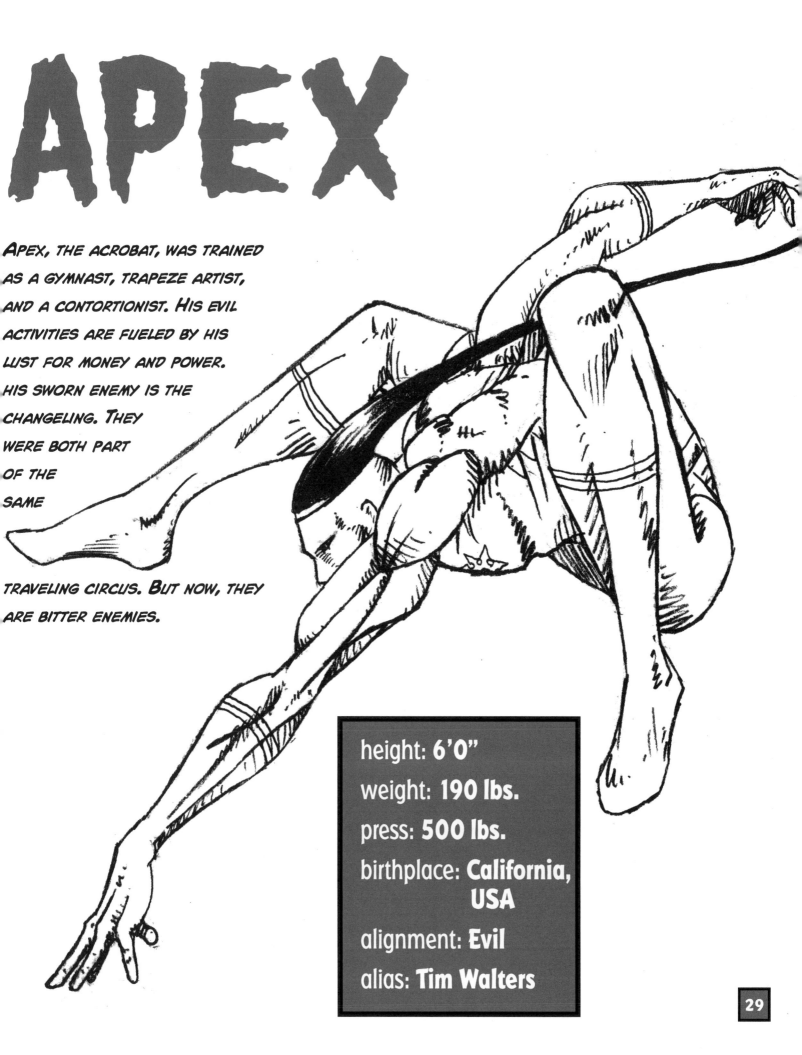

height: **6'0"**

weight: **190 lbs.**

press: **500 lbs.**

birthplace: **California, USA**

alignment: **Evil**

alias: **Tim Walters**

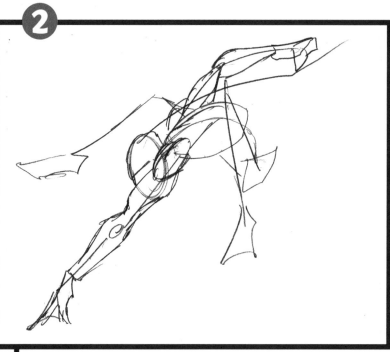

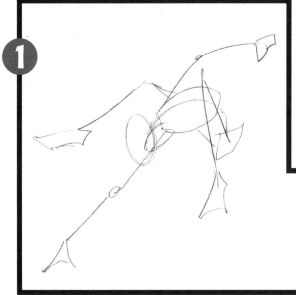

BEGIN BY DRAWING APEX AS HE LEAPS INTO ACTION. HE CAN BEND HIS BODY IN WAYS THAT REGULAR PEOPLE CAN-NOT. START BY SKETCHING THE BASIC FORM. THEN, ADD THE MUSCLES OF THE ARMS AND HANDS.

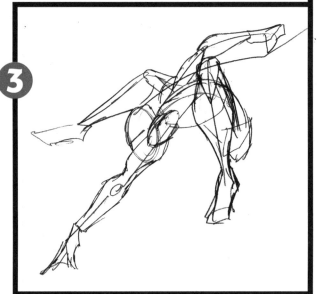

NEXT, ADD THE MUSCLES OF THE LEGS, AND DEFINE THE FEET AND HANDS. USE THE GUIDELINES ON THE FACE TO DRAW THE FA-CIAL FEATURES.

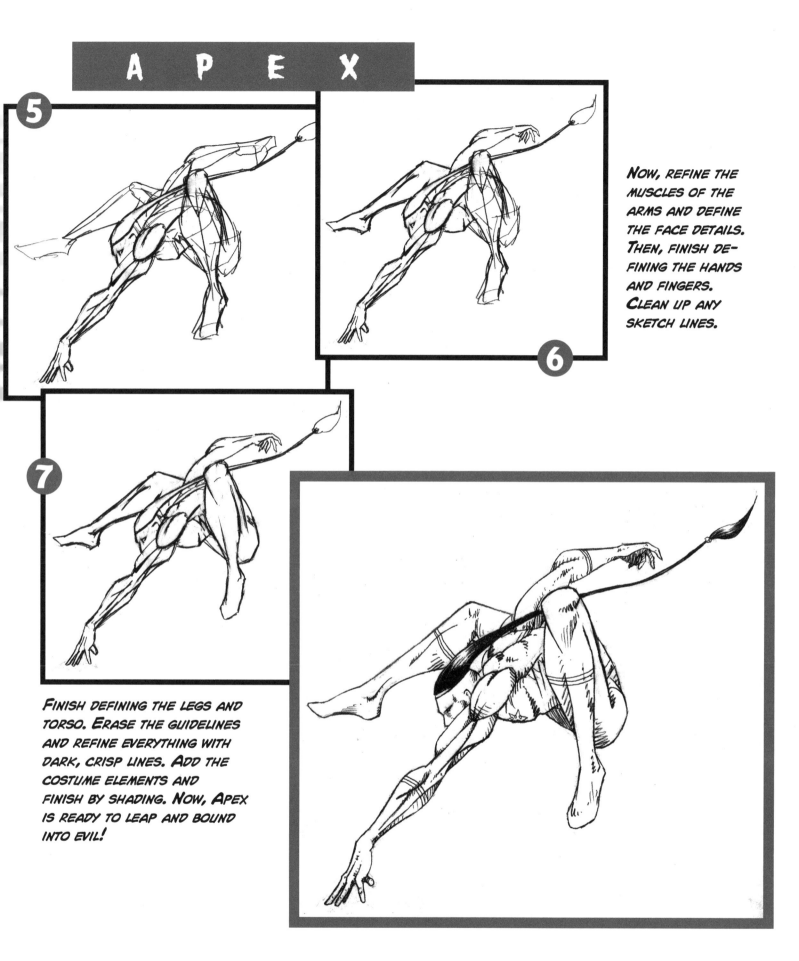

5

6

Now, refine the muscles of the arms and define the face details. Then, finish defining the hands and fingers. Clean up any sketch lines.

7

Finish defining the legs and torso. Erase the guidelines and refine everything with dark, crisp lines. Add the costume elements and finish by shading. Now, Apex is ready to leap and bound into evil!

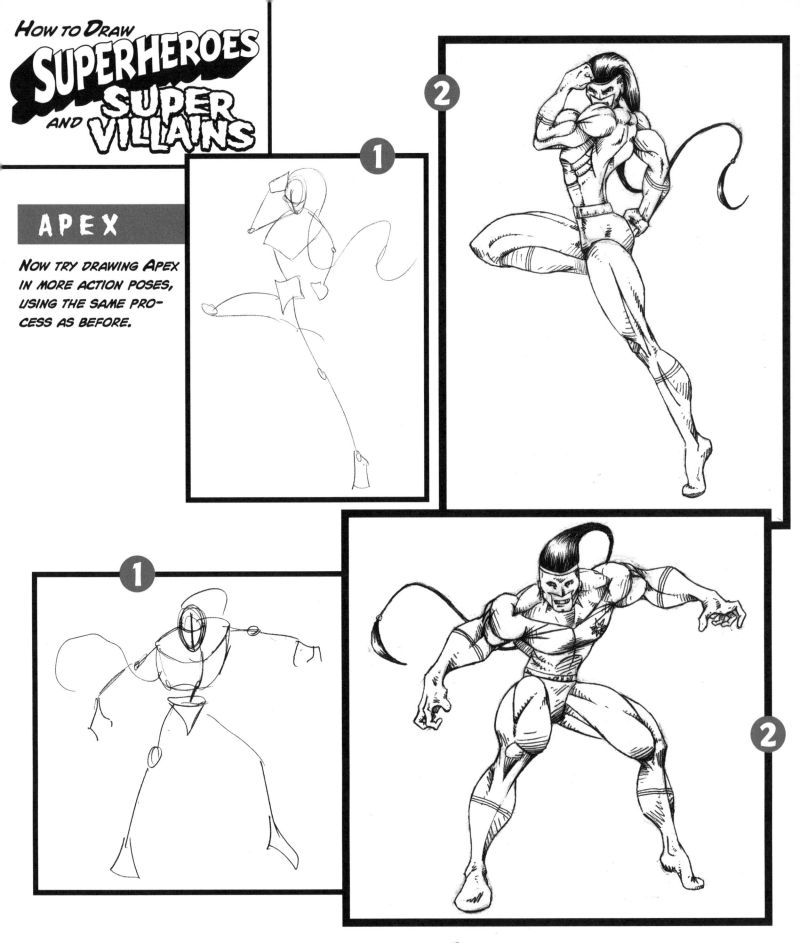

HOW TO DRAW SUPERHEROES AND SUPER VILLAINS

APEX

NOW TRY DRAWING APEX IN MORE ACTION POSES, USING THE SAME PROCESS AS BEFORE.

FOR THIS POSE, DRAW THE BASIC SKELETON, AS BEFORE. THEN DRAW AND DEFINE THE MUSCLES OF THE ARMS, LEGS, AND BODY. REFINE THESE AREAS AND ERASE THE FOUNDATION SKETCHES. THEN, CLEAN UP THE IMAGE WITH CLEAN LINES. TO FINISH APEX, ADD SOME SHADING AND HIS COSTUME DETAILS.

LIGER

John Nelson was a well-known scientist, studying endangered species. There was a horrible explosion in his lab, where dangerous chemicals mixed, and fused him with his favorite specimen, the Bengal tiger. The new creature, Liger, has the intelligence of John Nelson and the strength of a tiger. Liger is an extremely powerful creature and has joined with others to help protect the endangered species of the world.

height: **9'6"**
weight: **850 lbs.**
press: **20 tons**
birthplace: **Sydney, Australia**
alignment: **Good**
alias: **John Nelson**

33

HOW TO DRAW SUPERHEROES AND SUPER VILLAINS

Begin by drawing Liger in a crouching position, starting with the basic skeleton. Next, add the arm muscles.

Then, draw the leg muscles, and sketch the basic features of the face. Refine the hands and fingers.

5

6

Now, erase the foundation sketch of the face and refine the details of the head. Next, refine the arms and hands. Erase the foundation sketch and clean up all the lines.

7

Do the same for the legs and feet. Erase stray lines and finalize the sketch. To finish the mighty Liger, add some whiskers and shading.

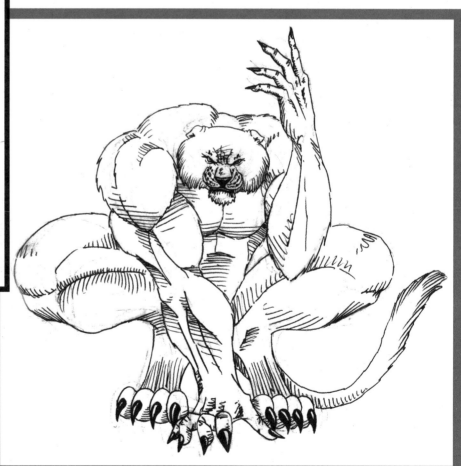

LIGER

HERE ARE SOME ALTERNATE POSITIONS FOR LIGER. FIRST DRAW LIGER IN A POUNCING POSITION, STARTING WITH THE BASIC SKELETON.

1

2

1

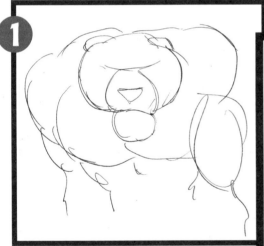

2

DRAW A CLOSE-UP OF LIGER. START BY SKETCHING THE HEAD AND TORSO. THEN ADD THE MUSCLES OF THE ARMS. DEFINE THESE AREAS, AND LIGHTLY ERASE THE SKETCH. NOW DRAW CLEAN, DARK LINES TO FINALIZE THE FACE AND BODY. ADD SOME LINES FOR SHADOW AND SOME WHISKERS TO FINISH THE DRAWING.

QUEEN ALLISETTE

QUEEN ALLISETTE COMES FROM AN AMAZON TRIBE IN SOUTH AMERICA, WHERE SHE IS WORSHIPPED. HOWEVER, SHE CHOOSES THE PATH OF EVIL. HER GOALS ARE TO CONQUER AND DOMINATE THE WORLD. WITH HER AWESOME MAGICAL STAFF SHE WEAKENS THE POWERS OF THOSE WHO OPPOSE HER.

height: **6'1"**
weight: **140 lbs.**
press: **175 lbs.**
birthplace: **Iquitos, Peru**
alignment: **Evil**
alias: **Allisette Leiva**

BEGIN DRAWING QUEEN ALLISETTE AS SHE WEILDS HER MAGICAL STAFF. START BY DRAWING A BASIC SKELETON. NEXT, DRAW THE MUSCLES OF THE ARMS AND TORSO.

THEN, DRAW THE MUSCLES OF THE STOMACH AND LEGS. DEFINE THE MAGICAL STAFF, AND USE THE GUIDELINES ON THE OVAL TO SKETCH THE FACIAL FEATURES.

5

6

Continue to refine the face. Then, erase the foundation sketch, and finalize the facial features, staff, and arms.

7

Now, erase the foundation sketch on the legs and cape. Refine these areas using dark, clean lines. Finalize the drawing by adding the costume details and shading. Now, Allisette looks ready for trouble.

QUEEN ALLISETTE

Now, draw Allisette in some alternate positions. Start with a close-up, drawing the oval for the head. Add the guidelines to define the placement of the eyes, nose, and mouth. Then, sketch the neck and shoulders. Refine all of these areas and lightly erase the sketch foundation. Now clean up the drawing by using dark lines. Finish the drawing with added costume details and shading.

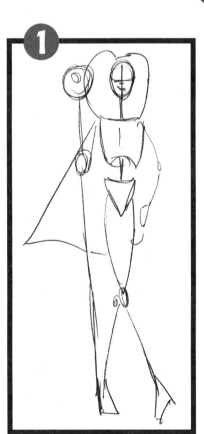

Now try this pose. Start by sketching the basic human skeleton, and follow the same steps from previous pages.

CHANGELING

BEFORE HE WAS THE CHANGELING, DAVID FERRIS WAS A CIRCUS PERFORMER. HE AND ARCH ENEMY, APEX, WERE PARTNERS IN THE SAME SHOW. A MYSTERIOUS ACCIDENT CHANGED FERRIS' LIFE FOREVER. APEX WAS JEALOUS OF FERRIS' ABILITY AND SALARY, SO HE POISONED HIS FOOD WITH INDUSTRIAL WASTE. THE MUTATING AGENT GAVE FERRIS THE SUPERHUMAN ABILITY TO CHANGE HIS COLOR AND TRANSFORM INTO ANY ANIMAL. THE CHANGELING HAS VOWED TO DO ANYTHING HE CAN TO STOP APEX.

height: **5'9"**

weight: **160 lbs.**

press: **400 lbs.**

birthplace: **California, USA**

alignment: **Good**

alias: **David Lee Ferris**

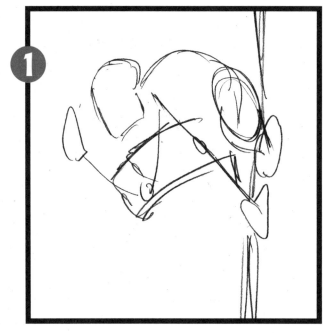

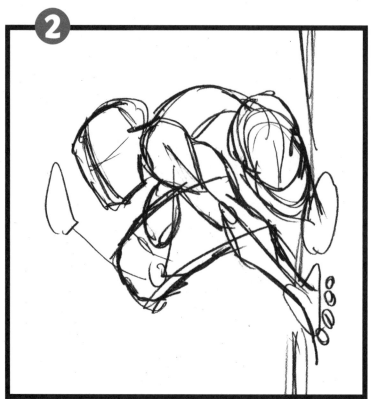

BEGIN DRAWING THE CHANGELING IN AN ACROBATIC POSE. START BY SKETCHING THE BASIC SKELETON. NEXT, ADD THE MUSCLES OF THE ARMS AND BACK.

USE GUIDELINES TO SHOW THE FACIAL FEATURES. ADD THE MUSCLES OF THE LEGS. DEFINE THE TAIL AREA. START CLEANING UP THE IMAGE.

5

6

REFINE THE FACE
AND NECK AREAS.
DEFINE THE HANDS
AND ARMS. ERASE
THE FOUNDATION
SKETCH AND REFINE
THESE AREAS.

7

NEXT, ERASE THE FOUNDATION SKETCH OF
THE LEGS AND BACK. REFINE THESE AREAS
WITH CLEAN, DARK LINES. ADD ANY REMAINING
COSTUME DETAILS AND SHADING TO FINISH THE
DRAWING. NOW THE CHANGELING CAN JUMP
INTO ACTION!

Now, draw the Changeling in some action poses. Try this downward leap starting with the basic skeleton.

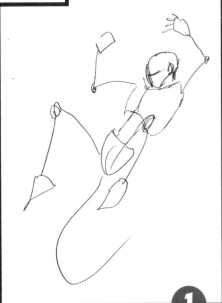

1

2

1

2

Next, pose him in a one-arm hand-stand. Begin by drawing the basic human form, and add the muscles to the whole figure. Next refine these areas including the face. Then, erase the figure and finalize with clean, crisp lines. Add the remaing costume details and shading.

44

HAMMERHEAD

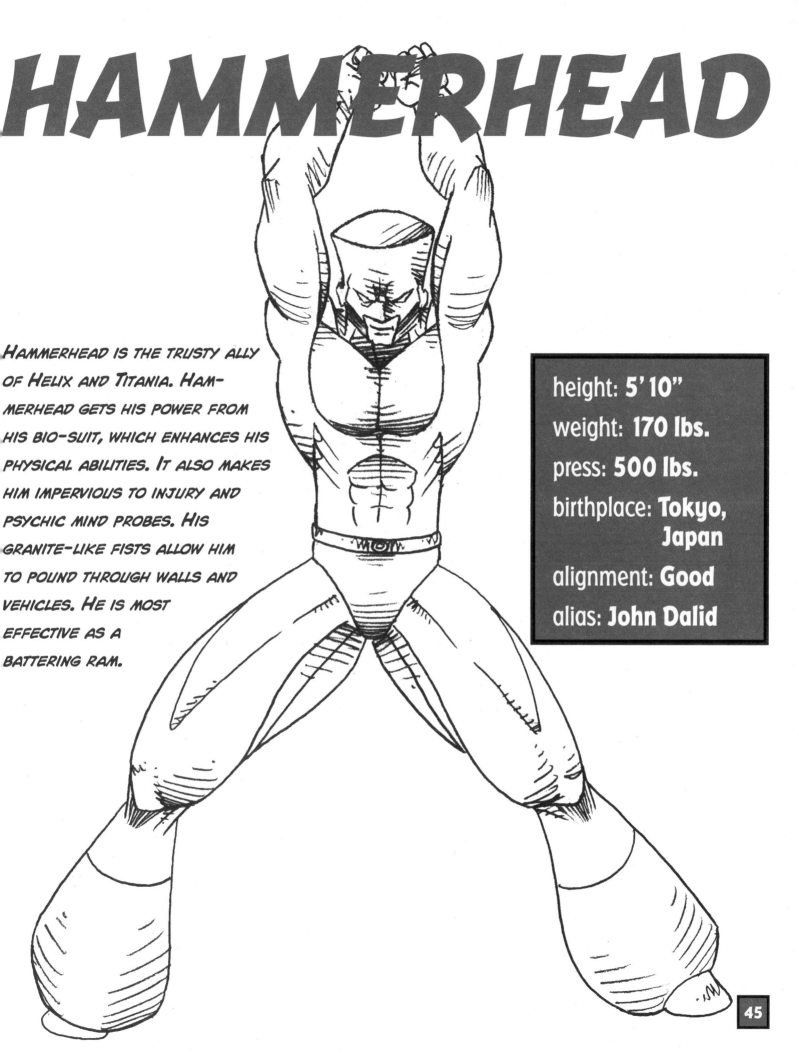

Hammerhead is the trusty ally of Helix and Titania. Hammerhead gets his power from his bio-suit, which enhances his physical abilities. It also makes him impervious to injury and psychic mind probes. His granite-like fists allow him to pound through walls and vehicles. He is most effective as a battering ram.

height: **5' 10"**
weight: **170 lbs.**
press: **500 lbs.**
birthplace: **Tokyo, Japan**
alignment: **Good**
alias: **John Dalid**

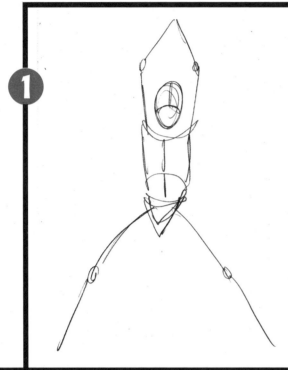

1

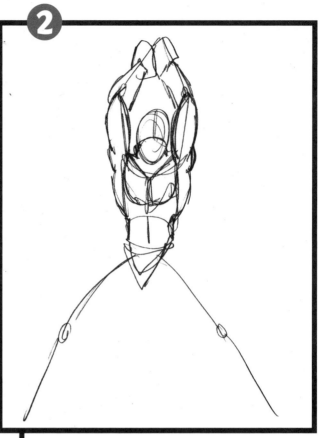

2

Draw Hammerhead as he gets ready to deliver a double-fisted blow. Draw the basic skeleton. Then, add the muscles of the body and arms.

3

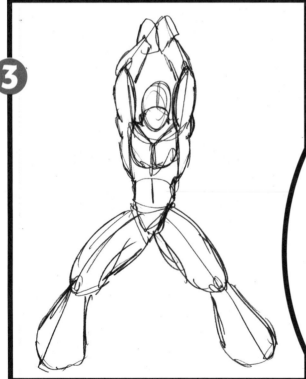

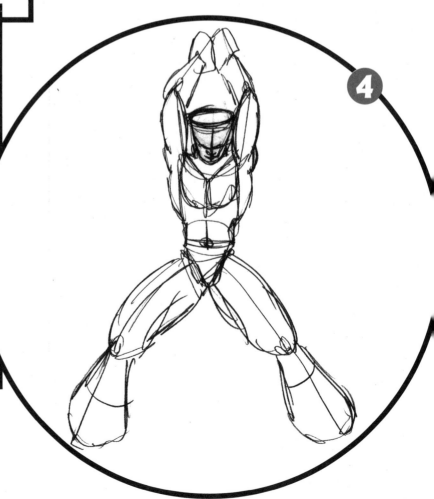

4

Next, add the waist and the muscles of the legs. Use the guidelines to refine the facial features. Refine the neck area, as well.

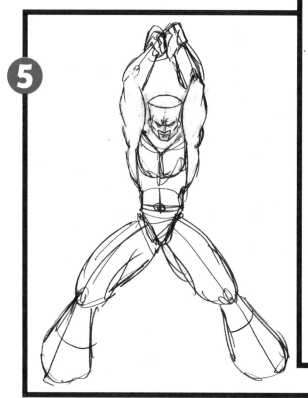

5

6

Now, erase the foundation sketch for the head and shoulders. Refine these areas with clean lines. Do the same for the torso, arms, and fists.

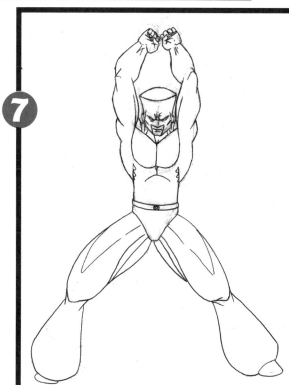

7

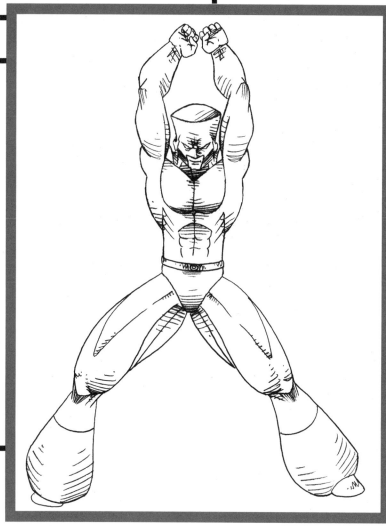

Next, erase the foundation sketch for the waist and legs. Clean up these areas using dark, crisp lines. Finally, add shading and finish the costume details to make Hammerhead come to life.

HOW TO DRAW SUPERHEROES AND SUPER VILLAINS

Now, try to draw Hammerhead in some other poses. Begin by drawing a close-up. Draw the basic oval face and define the shoulders. Next, refine the facial features, erase the foundation sketch, and refine the entire image with clean lines. Finally, add some muscle lines for intenstiy. Finish the costume, and add some shading.

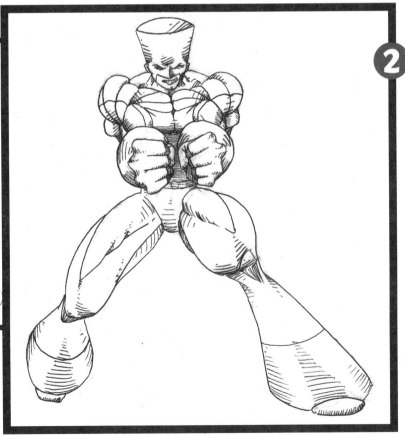

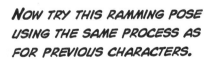

Now try this ramming pose using the same process as for previous characters.

STILETTO
AND MONSTROSITY

STILETTO AND HER MINION, MONSTROSITY, ARE TWO OF THE MOST DIABOLICAL MINDS ON EARTH. THEY ARE FROM ANOTHER WORLD WHERE THEY USE PORTALS TO UNLEASH THEIR UNSPEAKABLE HORRORS TO CONQUER OTHER WORLDS. THEY MUST BOTH BE TOGETHER ON EARTH OR THEIR POWERS WILL DIMINISH. TOGETHER THEY ARE SEEMINGLY INVINCIBLE.

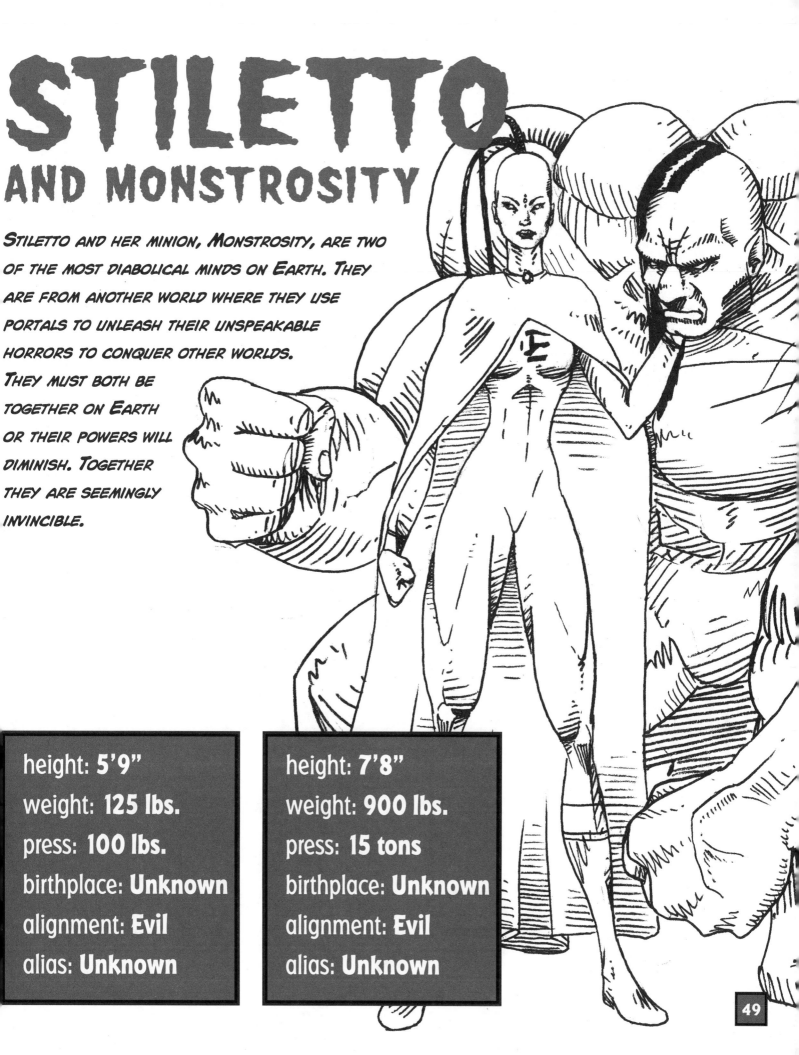

height: **5'9"**
weight: **125 lbs.**
press: **100 lbs.**
birthplace: **Unknown**
alignment: **Evil**
alias: **Unknown**

height: **7'8"**
weight: **900 lbs.**
press: **15 tons**
birthplace: **Unknown**
alignment: **Evil**
alias: **Unknown**

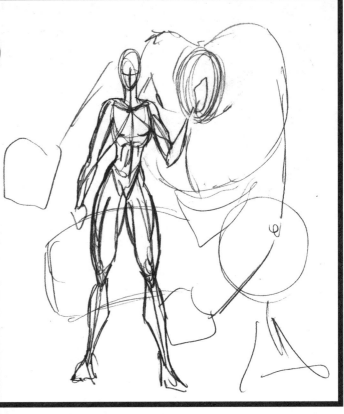

2

1

Begin drawing this dastardly duo with the basic skeleton. Next, add Stiletto's arms, legs, and torso.

3

4

Add the muscle to Monstrosity's skeleton. Define the arms, legs, and torso. Use the guidelines on the head to refine the facial features.

5

6

ADD MORE DETAIL TO THE FACIAL FEATURES. THEN, ERASE AND REFINE THE FACES USING CLEAN, CRISP LINES. ERASE THE FOUNDATION SKETCHES OF STILETTO'S TORSO AND MONSTROSITY'S RIGHT ARM. REFINE THESE AREAS WITH DARK, CLEAN LINES.

7

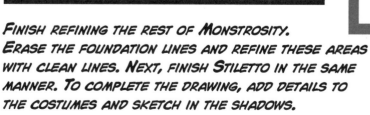

FINISH REFINING THE REST OF MONSTROSITY. ERASE THE FOUNDATION LINES AND REFINE THESE AREAS WITH CLEAN LINES. NEXT, FINISH STILETTO IN THE SAME MANNER. TO COMPLETE THE DRAWING, ADD DETAILS TO THE COSTUMES AND SKETCH IN THE SHADOWS.

STILETTO AND MONSTROSITY

Now draw these two villains in other poses. As always, start with the basic skeleton for Monstrosity. Add the muscles of the arms, legs, and body. Refine these areas, including the face. Next erase the foundation sketch and clean up the image with dark, crisp lines. To finish, add the remaining costume details and shading.

Now draw Stiletto as she gets ready to attack, following the same steps detailed on the preceeding pages.

PHOENICIA

Phoenicia is a martial arts expert. She has been studying martial arts since the age of 8, when Master Fong adopted her after her parents were mysteriously killed. She wields many different weapons, but her weapon of choice is nunchuks. Now, she polices the streets with vigilante justice, looking for clues to her parent's death.

height: **5'7"**

weight: **140 lbs.**

press: **200 lbs.**

birthplace: **New York, New York**

alignment: **Good**

alias: **Pam Hayden**

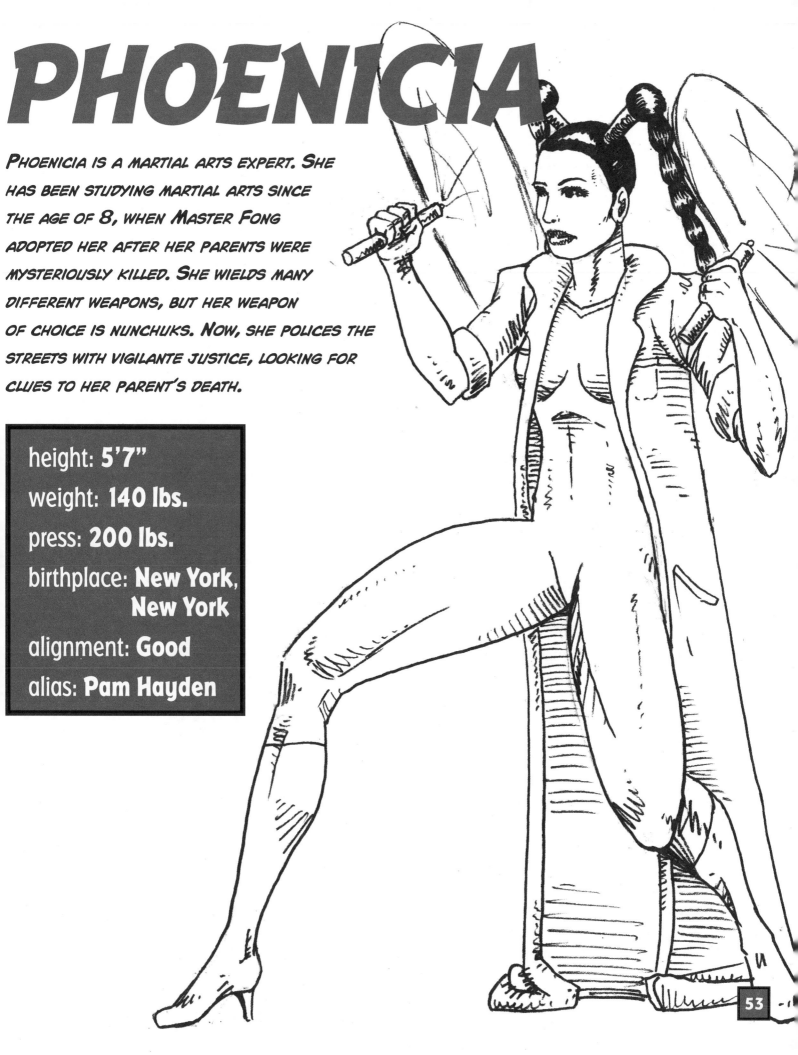

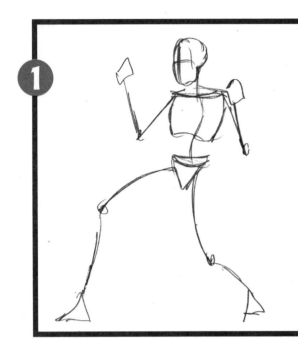

DRAW PHOENICIA DEMONSTRATING HER WEAPON TECHNIQUES. DRAW THE BASIC HUMAN SKELETON. NEXT, ADD THE MUSCLES OF THE ARMS AND TORSO.

THEN, DRAW THE MUSCLES OF HER LEGS AND WAIST. ADD THE NUNCHUKS. USING THE GUIDELINES OF THE FACE, DEFINE THE EYES, NOSE, AND MOUTH. ADD THE HAIR.

5

6

Now erase the foundation sketch of the face. Then refine the face and head with clean lines. Next, do the same for the arms and torso.

7

Now erase the foundation sketching of the legs. Redefine the areas of the legs using clean and crisp lines. To finalize the drawing, add any remaing costume elements and shading.

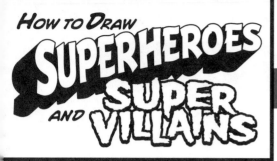

PHOENICIA

TRY DRAWING PHOENICIA IN ALTERNATE POSES. START WITH A CLOSE-UP OF HER FACE. BEGIN BY DRAWING THE OVAL FOR THE HEAD AND THE GUIDELINES TO PLACE THE EYES, NOSE, AND MOUTH. THEN, REFINE THE FACIAL FEATURES. NEXT, ERASE THE FOUNDATION SKETCH, AND CLEAN-UP THE IMAGE. FINALIZE YOUR DRAWING WITH SHADING AND COSTUME DETAILS.

OR TRY THIS POSE STARTING WITH THE BASIC SKELETON FORM.

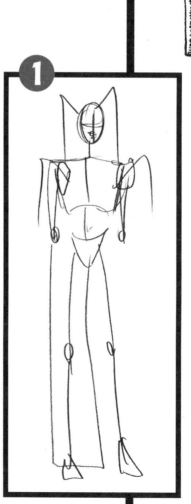

PHAROAH

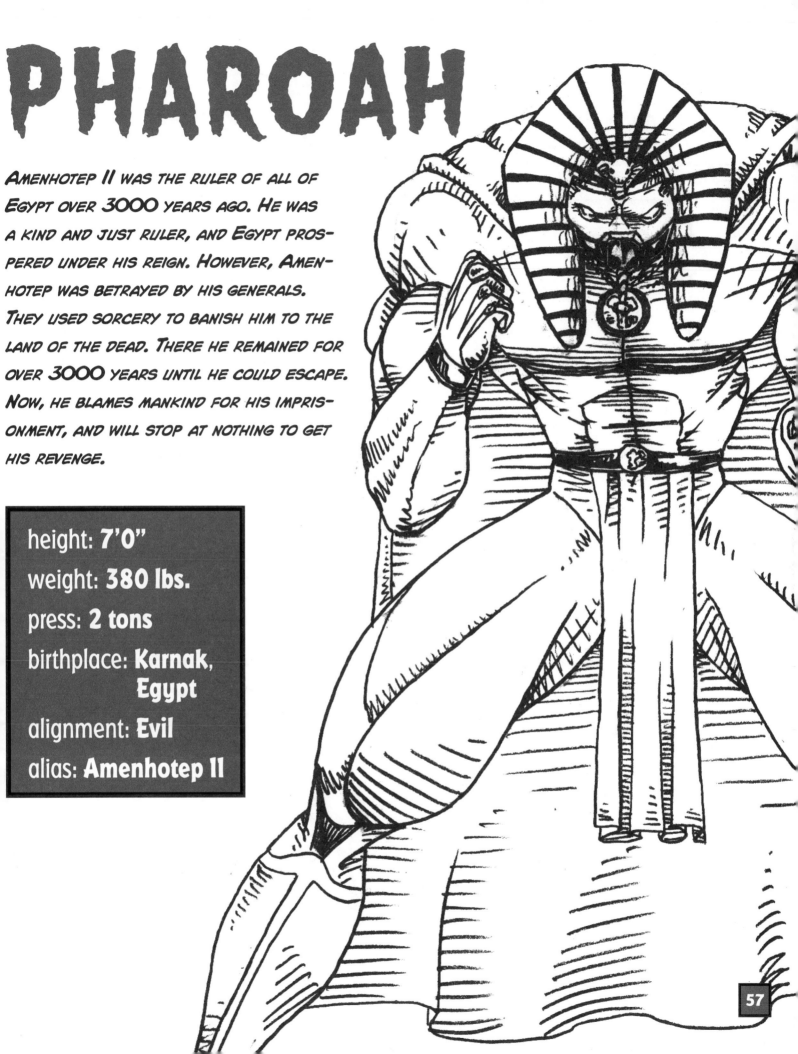

AMENHOTEP II WAS THE RULER OF ALL OF EGYPT OVER 3000 YEARS AGO. HE WAS A KIND AND JUST RULER, AND EGYPT PROSPERED UNDER HIS REIGN. HOWEVER, AMENHOTEP WAS BETRAYED BY HIS GENERALS. THEY USED SORCERY TO BANISH HIM TO THE LAND OF THE DEAD. THERE HE REMAINED FOR OVER 3000 YEARS UNTIL HE COULD ESCAPE. NOW, HE BLAMES MANKIND FOR HIS IMPRISONMENT, AND WILL STOP AT NOTHING TO GET HIS REVENGE.

height: **7'0"**
weight: **380 lbs.**
press: **2 tons**
birthplace: **Karnak, Egypt**
alignment: **Evil**
alias: **Amenhotep II**

HOW TO DRAW SUPERHEROES AND SUPER VILLAINS

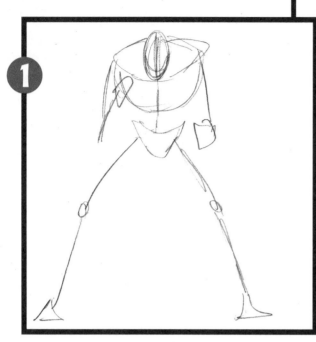

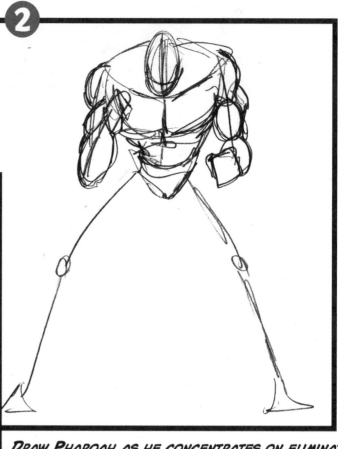

DRAW PHAROAH AS HE CONCENTRATES ON ELIMINATING HIS ENEMIES. START WITH THE BASIC HUMAN SKELETON. NEXT, ADD THE MUSCLE MASS ON HIS ARMS AND TORSO.

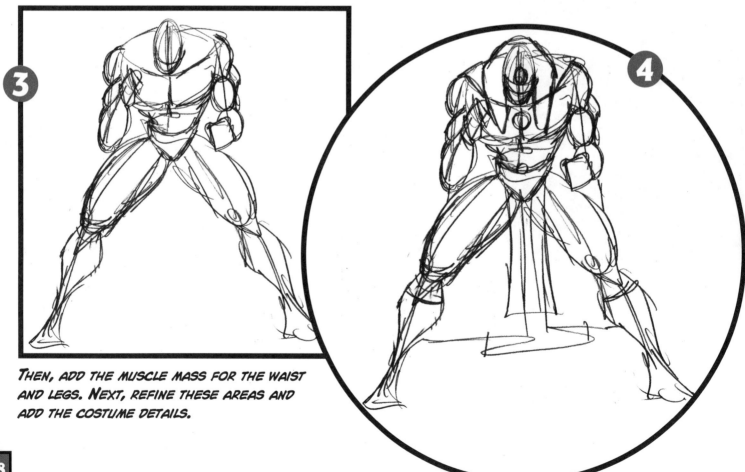

THEN, ADD THE MUSCLE MASS FOR THE WAIST AND LEGS. NEXT, REFINE THESE AREAS AND ADD THE COSTUME DETAILS.

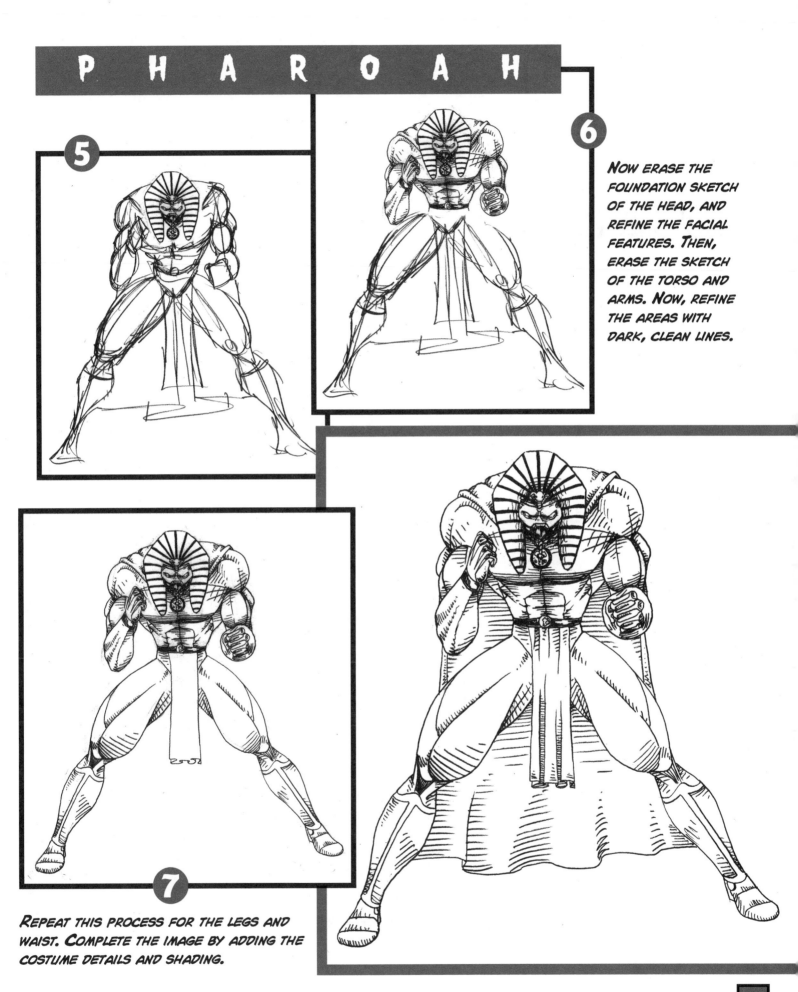

5

6

NOW ERASE THE FOUNDATION SKETCH OF THE HEAD, AND REFINE THE FACIAL FEATURES. THEN, ERASE THE SKETCH OF THE TORSO AND ARMS. NOW, REFINE THE AREAS WITH DARK, CLEAN LINES.

7

REPEAT THIS PROCESS FOR THE LEGS AND WAIST. COMPLETE THE IMAGE BY ADDING THE COSTUME DETAILS AND SHADING.

HOW TO DRAW SUPERHEROES AND SUPER VILLAINS

PHAROAH

NOW, DRAW SOME ALTER-NATE POSES OF PHAROAH. BEGIN BY DRAWING THE BASIC HUMAN SKELETON. THEN, ADD THE MUSCLES OF THE TORSO, ARMS, AND LEGS. REFINE THESE AREAS AND LIGHTLY ERASE. CLEAN UP THE DRAWING WITH DARK LINES. FINISH THE IMAGE WITH SOME SHADING AND COSTUME DETAIL.

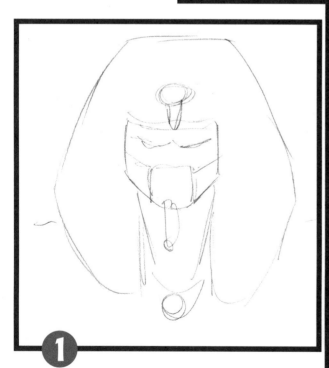

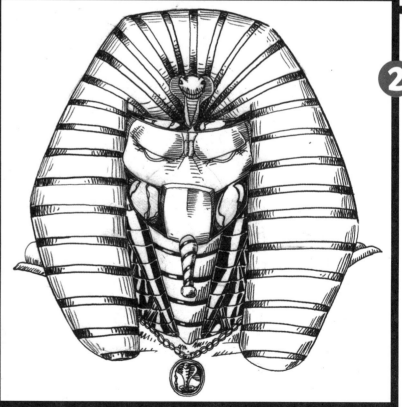

NOW TRY A CLOSE-UP OF PHAROAH'S MASK.

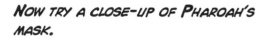

HYPERION

By day, Jerry David is a mild-mannered weatherman for Channel Six news. By night, he is the superhero known as Hyperion. Hyperion was born on Jupiter's moon, Titan. He could not allow the rampant crime on Earth to continue. On Earth, his super powers are almost limitless, making him the most powerful being in the galaxy.

height: **6'6"**
weight: **250 lbs.**
press: **5 tons**
birthplace: **Titan**
alignment: **Good**
alias: **Jerry David**

HOW TO DRAW SUPERHEROES AND SUPER VILLAINS

1

2

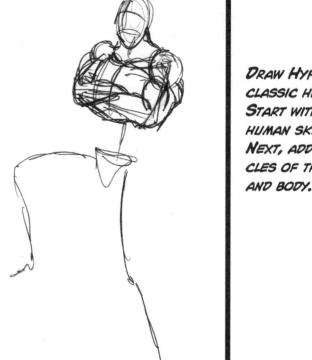

DRAW HYPERION IN A CLASSIC HERO POSE. START WITH THE BASIC HUMAN SKELETON. NEXT, ADD THE MUSCLES OF THE ARMS AND BODY.

3

4

THEN, ADD THE MUSLES FOR THE LEGS. REFINE THESE AREAS. NEXT, ADD THE COSTUME AND FACIAL DETAILS.

5

6

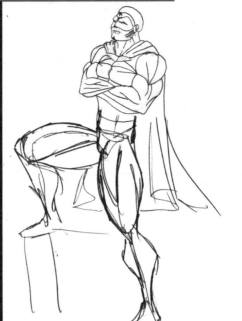

NEXT, ERASE THE FOUNDATION SKETCH OF THE FACE AND HEAD. THEN REFINE THESE AREAS WITH CLEAN, CRISP LINES. DO THE SAME FOR HYPERION'S ARMS AND BODY.

7

NEXT ERASE THE FOUNDATION LINES FOR THE LEGS AND WAIST. CLEAN UP THESE AREAS, THEN DEFINE WITH DARK, CRISP LINES. TO FINISH THE IMAGE, ADD ANY REMAINING COSTUME ELEMENTS AND SHADING FOR EFFECT.

HYPERION

DRAW SOME ALTERNATE POSES OF HYPERION. AS ALWAYS, START WITH THE BASIC SKELETON. NEXT, ADD THE MUSCLES OF THE TORSO, ARMS, AND LEGS. REFINE THESE AREAS AND LIGHTLY ERASE. THEN, USE CLEAN AND DARK LINES TO DEFINE THE IMAGE. FINISH BY ADDING THE REMAINING COSTUME DETAILS AND SHADING.

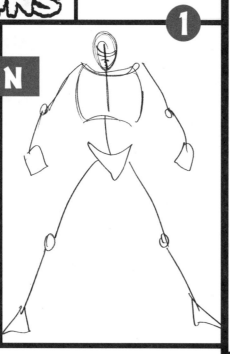

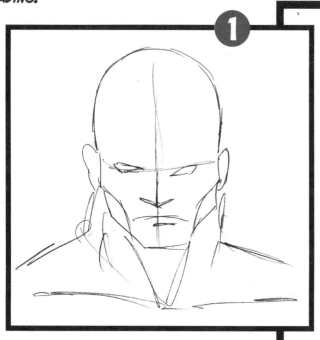

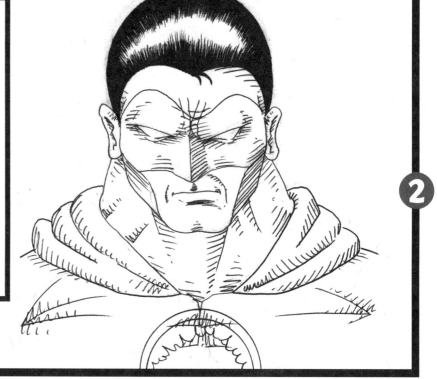

MAKE THE SECOND POSE A CLOSE-UP. DRAW THE OVAL FOR THE HEAD AND GUIDELINES FOR THE FACIAL FEATURES. REFINE THESE FEATURES AND LIGHTLY ERASE. NEXT REFINE THE FACE USING CLEAN LINES. FINISH THE DRAWING BY ADDING THE COSTUME AND SHADING DETAILS.